Gold Rush Adventure

by **Adam Guillain**

illustrated by Giuliano Aloisi

a Capstone company — publishers for children

Engage Literacy is published in the UK by Raintree.
Raintree is an imprint of Capstone Global Library Limited, a company
incorporated in England and Wales having its registered office at 264 Banbury
Road, Oxford, OX2 7DY – Registered company number: 6695582

www.raintree.co.uk

10 9 8 7 6 5 4 3 2
Printed in India.

Gold Rush Adventure

ISBN: 978-1-4747-1786-1

CONTENTS

Chapter 1

Life on the farm

Kenda and Aman lived with their father and grandma on a small farm. Every day before breakfast, Kenda and Aman fed the chickens and collected the eggs. Sometimes Grandma brought another basket and joined them.

"Don't put all your eggs in one basket," she joked. "You might end up with no eggs at all if you drop them."

It was always fried eggs and bread for breakfast.

"Come and get it!" Grandma called. The eggs were ready. "Sunny-side up and crisp and golden."

"All right everyone," Father often said when everyone had eaten. "Let's get to work."

Father took care of the crops and getting the corn to the miller to have it ground into flour. It was Kenda's job to milk the cow, then look after the horse, Dewdrop. Kenda loved this job and talked about Dewdrop all the time. Aman, on the other hand, had to feed the fat pig and clean the pen.

"Why do I get the hard jobs?" he would mutter.

Farm life was sometimes difficult, but the children were happy.

"As long as we have corn, we can pay the rent on the farm," said Grandma. She liked to remind everyone of this from time to time, usually when she was baking.

There was always enough money to buy meat, new clothes and sometimes even colourful sweets.

When all the jobs were done, the children returned to the kitchen for their lessons.

"Today we are going to learn about money," said Grandma one day. She then took several coins from an old tin. As the children practised their adding and subtracting, Grandma talked.

"The farm is very important because it is how we make our money," she said. "But there is more to life than money. As long as we have eggs to cook and corn to sell, we'll be fine."

Aman knew Grandma was right. But he couldn't help wishing for more.

"Life would be much better with more money," he whispered to Kenda. "And why not dream for more than eggs and bread? A life with riches. Now, that would be amazing."

Chapter 2

GOLDEN DREAMS

The next day, the children and their father met a woman walking past their farm.

"Have you heard the story?" she asked them. "They say a man with a donkey and a small sack of tools and food went to look for gold in the mountains." The woman laughed.

"Well, at least he has dreams," said Father.

That night, Father returned to the farm with news.

"That man with the donkey," he told them. "He's called a prospector, and guess what? He found gold in the mountains! If we had luck like that we could finally own our own farm!"

The gold rush had started. Shopkeepers, workers, and farmers dropped everything and hurried for the mountains.

"I think we should join the gold rush. It will be a great family adventure. What do you say, kids?" Father asked Aman and Kenda one night. "We must all go soon."

"But it's almost time for the harvest," said Grandma. "If you don't harvest the corn, it may go bad, and we won't be able to sell it!"

"And who will feed the pig?" asked Aman.

"We'll have to sell the pig to buy the things we need," Father answered.

"Well, you can leave me here with the chickens," said Grandma. "Chasing gold is a fool's game."

Grandma was very upset that night, but Father was excited about their gold rush adventure. Kenda and Aman, however, felt nervous but excited.

"If we find gold, I won't have to do the hard chores anymore," said Aman.

"And I might even have my own beautiful horse," said Kenda.

Father sold the pig and bought a cart, shovels, and three sieves. The sieves were special pans to sift gold from dirt in the river water. He then bought enough food to last them a month.

One beautiful, sunny morning in spring, Kenda and Aman set off with their father to the mountains.

Chapter 3

THE RUSH

"I don't like this," said Aman as he drove the horse and cart. "There are so many carts and horses on the road. How are we ever going to find our own place to look for gold? Too many others are trying to do the same thing."

By nightfall, the three prospectors had stopped their cart by a tree near the river.

"Kenda, please take care of the horse," said Father. "Aman, can you help me with the fire?"

That night they ate beans from a pan and drank fresh, clean water from the river.

"Father," said Kenda, "what will we do if all the gold is gone?"

"We haven't even started yet," said Father. "There's gold in those mountains. I can feel it. Let's give it a try. It will be a great adventure!"

That night they slept under the wooden cart.

The children awoke at dawn to the sound of frying eggs.

"Come and get it," their father called. "Sunny-side up and crisp and golden."

Hearing Father say Grandma's old words made the children feel much better. They sat happily eating, until they had all finished.

"All right, everyone. Let's get to work," said Father.

That morning, they panned for gold in the shallows where the river water was low. Aman thought about his grandma. He wondered if she was even now feeding the chickens. "Don't put all your eggs in one basket," she liked to say. Aman smiled when he thought of this. But then he wondered. What if they were putting all their eggs in one basket coming here to find gold?

By the end of that first day, all they had to show for their hard work were arms that hurt.

"Panning for gold is hard work," moaned Aman.

"You both did a great job today. Each day will get easier," Father said. "But if we discover gold, we'll be able to have a better life."

Kenda didn't feel quite so sure. What if they didn't discover any gold? Even now, the corn at home was ready to harvest. If it went bad in the ground, what would they do for money?

Chapter 4

THE LONG WALK HOME

Four weeks passed. The banks of the river were getting crowded with other prospectors.

"I'm tired of eating red beans every day," Aman told his sister.

"I wish we had fresh eggs to eat," Kenda replied.

Several times, one or more of them had been ready to give up. But then they would hear a new story.

22

"I heard a woman upstream found some gold nuggets," said one man.

"A family downstream also struck gold and became rich!" said another. There were other wonderful stories, too.

One morning, during the fifth week, something very exciting happened.

"Look!" Kenda gasped. She was peering into her pan. "Gold!" It was only a few yellow flakes, but her heart was pounding with excitement.

By the end of that week, all three of them had found a few flakes of gold.

"Are we rich?" Aman asked his father.

"Not rich," said Father, "But this gold will help us pay the rent on the farm for the next few months. It might even be enough to buy another pig."

"And another horse?" asked Kenda, hopefully.

"We'll see," said Father with a smile.

Sadly, by the end of that week, there were too many prospectors looking for gold. It was impossible to find a new place to sift in.

"I think it's time we returned home," Father suggested.

Right after breakfast the next morning, they started the long journey home.

Back on the farm, Grandma had just finished collecting the eggs when she saw them coming down the road. By now much of the crop had gone bad, and a small part of her wanted to be angry. But she wasn't.

"You're just in time for breakfast," she cried with joy.

"Oh Grandma, we missed you so much!" Kenda cried. Then everyone hugged each other tight.

29

"And are we rich?" Grandma asked her son.

"We have a little gold," said Father. "But more importantly, we have each other. That's rich enough for me."

As they ate their eggs and bread, the children told Grandma the story of their adventure. After that, to everyone's amazement, Grandma told her own story. The story of how she alone had harvested what little of the crop she could. It wasn't much, but it was something. She had then taken some of the corn to the miller.

"I told him to pay me in flour," she told them. "I also have some seed for the next planting. It's not gold, but it is valuable."

Father looked at Grandma proudly. "I wanted us to have riches beyond our wildest dreams," he said.

"Perhaps we already do," said Grandma.

"It's a good thing you stayed here and did all this work," said Aman.

"Well, you know what I say," said Grandma. "Don't put all your eggs in one basket."